YOUR KNOWLEDGE HAS VALUE

- We will publish your bachelor's and master's thesis, essays and papers

- Your own eBook and book - sold worldwide in all relevant shops

- Earn money with each sale

Upload your text at www.GRIN.com
and publish for free

Bibliographic information published by the German National Library:

The German National Library lists this publication in the National Bibliography; detailed bibliographic data are available on the Internet at http://dnb.dnb.de .

Imprint:

Copyright © 2010 GRIN Verlag, Open Publishing GmbH
Print and binding: Books on Demand GmbH, Norderstedt Germany
ISBN: 9783640622689

This book at GRIN:

http://www.grin.com/en/e-book/150362/financial-management

Arkadi Borowski

Financial Management

The role and importance of capital markets and EMH

GRIN Publishing

GRIN - Your knowledge has value

Since its foundation in 1998, GRIN has specialized in publishing academic texts by students, college teachers and other academics as e-book and printed book. The website www.grin.com is an ideal platform for presenting term papers, final papers, scientific essays, dissertations and specialist books.

Visit us on the internet:

http://www.grin.com/

http://www.facebook.com/grincom

http://www.twitter.com/grin_com

University of Sunderland

BA (HONS) BUSINESS MANAGEMENT

Financial Management

Module Title: Financial Management
Return date: Friday 8th January 2010
Arkadi Borowski

Germany

Index of contents

1. Task 1

The role and importance of capital markets and EMH

Crisp plc has to attract investments from capital markets.

A capital market is simply any market where a government or a company (usually a corporation) can raise money (capital) to fund their operations and long term (periods longer than a year) investment.[1] Usual, short-term funds can be founded on other markets (e.g., the money market). The capital market consists of the stock market (equity securities) and the bond market (debt). Bonds and stocks are two ways to generate capital of any company.

New issues of bonds and stocks are placed on primary capital markets by way of underwriting among investors. All money, received during underwriting, goes to company (Crisp plc) for its investment purposes.

And placed bonds and stocks are sold and bought among other investors or traders in the secondary capital markets (a securities exchange, over-the-counter, or elsewhere). The prices of securities (both bonds and stocks) on secondary markets are reflected «real» price of company. It is good benchmark for primary placements of additional issues of bonds and/or stocks (further extension of the company).

Crisp plc is going to issue bond or stocks. It means that it attract money from primary markets. Here very important thing is true price of bonds and/or stocks of Crisp plc, i.e. price has to be interesting for investors and allows to attract maximum of money.

As stated above, prices of securities on secondary markets are reflected «real» price of company from point of view of investors. Here the **efficient-market hypothesis (EMH)** plays very important role, because it is the tool of securities pricing of off-site investors (which are outside of the company).

According to the **efficient-market hypothesis (EMH)**, which was developed by Professor Eugene Fama, financial markets are «informationally efficient».[2] It means that prices on traded assets are «real» and already reflect all known information. Prices change to reflect new information (for example, new investment program of the company). Consequently,   it is impossible to consistently outperform the market by using any information that the market already knows. Information or *news* in the EMH is defined as anything that may affect prices that is unknowable in the present and thus appears randomly in the future.

The main precondition of the theory is that agents have rational expectations. It means, that prices of all agents are different (small and big), but average of all prices is «real» price. So, not all agents can be rational. Investors' reactions are random and follow a normal distribution pattern. So, mean of distribution is «real» price of assets.

There are three forms of the efficient market hypothesis:

1. The «**Weak**» **form** implicates that all past market prices and data are fully reflected in securities prices. Future prices cannot be predicted by analyzing price from the past. So, investor will not able to receive permanent profit in the long run on the base of past prices. Future price movements are determined entirely by information not contained in the price series. In this case applying of technical analysis in the long run is useless. Additional return can be received via fundamental analysis or insider information.

2. The «**Semistrong**» **form** implicates that all publicly available information is fully reflected in securities prices. Share prices adjust to publicly available new information very rapidly and in an unbiased fashion. Here, applying of fundamental and technical tools in the long run is useless. Participant can use insider information only.

3. The «**Strong**» **form** implicates that all information is fully reflected in securities prices. So, even insider information is not to be used.

The EMH was used for a long time. But now there are a lot of disclaimer of this theory.

For example, requirement that EMH is random means that there are not trends in the long run. And you don't have to use technical analysis. But there are a lot of researches, which demonstrate any market trends for a long time (several weeks, months, years).[3] Also, there is positive correlation between degree of trending and length of time period.[4] Probably, main requirement of EMH about Gaussian distribution of stock markets is wrong. It is described in researches of Mandelbrot, Benoit & Hudson, Richard L.[5] and Taleb, Nassim Nicholas.[6] In this case using of EMH for real life is not correct.

Other researches do not reject the EMH, but assert about existence of bias. The bias is some predictable human errors, which are made in the process of making investment decisions. That is why most investors prefer to buy growth stocks at expensive prices and not work with high-value stocks. Investigations of Dreman show that low P/E stocks have greater returns and confirm this theory about human errors. [7]

Ray Ball in his investigation explains higher returns of stocks as stocks with higher beta. [8] And his theory was accepted by the EMH. But this theory can not explain why stocks with poor returns («losers») have much higher average returns than stocks with high returns («winners») over the following period of the same number of years. [9] In the long run «losers» become «winners» and this situation contradicts the EMH. Stocks with poor returns («losers») have low «beta». But for confirmation of the EMH, stocks with poor returns have to have high «beta».[10]

Speculative economic bubbles are other examples of irrational behavior on the market.[11]

Scientific world hasn't made well-defined conclusion about the EMH. But all participant of the market use public information to make investment decisions. And large public company like Crisp plc has take into account the opinion of investors from capital markets. This opinion reflects expectation of markets participant about price of the firm. In turn, this price of the firm is checkpoint for owners of the company to estimate quantity of money, which can be attracted by issue of bonds and stocks. So, management of large public company has to care market by correct information about the company. It will allow have «real» price of the company on the capital market.

2. Task 2

The different sources of finance available to large companies and the impact on cost of capital

Capital market is potential possibility to attract funds outside of the company. But this possibility has price too. It is cost of capital.

The cost of capital for potential investors is «the expected return on a portfolio of all the company's existing securities». [11] Other words, players of capital markets define minimum return of new project of a company, which they want to receive. That is, the rate of return that a company would otherwise be able to earn at the same risk level as the investment that has been selected. For example, when an investor purchases stock in a company, he/she expects to see a return on that investment. Since the individual expects to get back more than his/her initial investment, the cost of capital is equal to this return that the investor receives, or the money that the company misses out on by selling its stock. Consequently, the expected return on capital must be greater than the cost of capital (minimal expected return).

The large public company like Crisp plc has 2 ways to attract funds: issue of bonds and stocks. So, a company's cost of capital is defined on base of both the cost of debt and the cost of equity.

The **cost of debt** is the effective rate that a company pays on its current debt. This can be measured in either before- or after-tax returns. However, because interest expense is deductible, the after-tax cost is used. In practice, the interest-rate paid by the company can be modeled as the risk-free rate plus a risk component (risk premium). The formula can be written as:

$$(Rf + credit\ risk\ rate)(1-T),$$

where T is the corporate tax rate and Rf is the risk free rate. [11] The cost of debt is computed by taking the rate on a risk free bond whose duration matches the term structure of the corporate debt, then adding a default premium. This default premium will rise as the amount of debt increases (since the risk rises as the amount of debt rises). Since in most cases debt expense is a deductible expense, the cost of debt is computed as an after tax cost to make it comparable with the cost of equity (earnings are after-tax as well).

A company will use various bonds, loans and other forms of debt, so this measure is useful for giving an idea as to the overall rate being paid by the company to use debt financing. Riskier companies generally have a higher cost of debt. So, this ratio can be used to compare companied between each other.

For companies with similar risk or credit ratings, the interest rate is largely exogenous. It means that Crisp plc can define its cost of capital from the capital market, because it is large public company. Other words, Crisp plc has public debt history yet.

The **cost of equity** is the return that stockholders of the company require. A firm's cost of equity represents the compensation that the market demands in exchange for owning the asset and bearing the risk of ownership. Similar to the cost of debt, the cost of equity is broadly defined as the risk-weighted projected return required by investors, where the return is largely unknown. The general formula is [11]:

Cost of equity = Risk free rate of return + Premium expected for risk

The cost of equity is therefore *inferred* by comparing the investment to other investments (comparables) with similar risk profiles to determine the «market» cost of equity.

There are several methods to define cost of equity (various models of general formula of stocks' cost):

1) The traditional formula for cost of equity (COE) is the dividend capitalization model [12]:

$$\text{Cost of Equity} = \frac{\text{Dividends per Share (for next year)}}{\text{Current Market Value of Stock}} + \text{Growth Rate of Dividends} \quad \text{or}$$

Expected Return = dividend yield + growth rate of dividends.

2) The capital asset pricing model (CAPM) is another method used to determine cost of equity. The market risk is normally characterized by the β parameter. Thus, the investors would expect (or demand) to receive [12]:

$$E_s = R_f + \beta_s (R_m - R_f). \quad \text{or}$$

The expected return (%) = risk-free return (%) + sensitivity to market risk * (historical return (%) - risk-free return (%))

Where E_s – the expected return for a security

R_f – the expected risk-free return in that market (government bond yield)

β_s – the sensitivity to market risk for the security

R_M – the historical return of the stock market/ equity market

$(R_M\text{-}R_f)$ – the risk premium of market assets over risk free assets.

Crisp plc is large public company, having credit history. It means that the management of the company can use both dividend capitalization and CAPM models to define cost of equity.

The next step is calculation of general cost of capital on the basis of cost of debt and cost of equity. For this purposes is used the weighted-average cost of capital (WACC). The WACC can also be used as a discount rate for a project's projected cashflows.

So, it is easy to define cost of capital for Crisp plc, because it is large public company. But the main question is choice between 2 ways (bond or stocks) to attract funds from capital market. Other word, the management of the company has to define the capital structure.

Capital Structure is a mix of a company's long-term debt, specific short-term debt, common equity and preferred equity. [13] The capital structure is how a firm finances its overall operations and growth by using different sources of funds.

Debt comes in the form of bond issues or long-term notes payable, while equity is classified as common stock, preferred stock or retained earnings. Short-term debt such as working capital requirements is also considered to be part of the capital structure.

A company's proportion of short and long-term debt is considered when analyzing capital structure. When people refer to capital structure they are most likely referring to a firm's debt-to-equity ratio, which provides insight into how risky a company is. Usually a company more heavily financed by debt poses greater risk, as this firm is relatively highly levered.

Debt/Equity Ratio is a measure of a company's financial leverage calculated by dividing its total liabilities by stockholders' equity. It indicates what proportion of equity and debt the company is using to finance its assets [14]:

Debt/Equity Ratio=Total Liabilities / Shareholders Equity

A high debt/equity ratio generally means that a company has been aggressive in financing its growth with debt. This can result in volatile earnings as a result of the additional interest expense.

If a lot of debt is used to finance increased operations (high debt to equity), the company could potentially generate more earnings than it would have without this outside financing. If this were to increase earnings by a greater amount than the debt cost (interest), then the shareholders benefit as more earnings are being spread among the same amount of shareholders. However, the cost of this debt financing may outweigh the return that the company generates on the debt through investment and business activities and become too much for the company to handle. This can lead to bankruptcy, which would leave shareholders with nothing.

The debt/equity ratio also depends on the industry in which the company operates. For example, capital-intensive industries such as auto manufacturing tend to have a debt/equity ratio above 2, while personal computer companies have a debt/equity of under 0.5.

Because of tax advantages on debt issuance, it will be cheaper to issue debt rather than new equity (this is only true for profitable firms, tax breaks are available only to profitable firms). At some point, however, the cost of issuing new debt will be greater than the cost of issuing new equity. This is because adding debt increases the default risk - and thus the interest rate that the company must pay in order to borrow money. By utilizing too much debt in its capital structure, this increased default risk can also drive up the costs for other sources (such as retained earnings and preferred stock) as well. Management must identify the "optimal mix" of financing – the capital structure where the cost of capital is minimized so that the firm's value can be maximized.

3. Task 3

The practical aspects of the dividend decision and a critical evaluation of the theories of relevance and irrelevance of dividends to share valuation

Dividend Policy is the policy a company uses to decide how much it will pay out to shareholders in dividends.

Lots of research and economic logic suggests that dividend policy is irrelevant (in theory).

Dividend Irrelevance Theory is a theory that investors are not concerned with a company's dividend policy since they can sell a portion of their portfolio of equities if they want cash. [15] The dividend irrelevance theory essentially indicates that an issuance of dividends should have little to no impact on stock price.

If a company pays out dividends, but an investor would prefer the money to be re-invested, then the investor can simply use the dividends to buy more shares.

Conversely, if a company retains too much (from a shareholder's point of view), then the share price will be boosted by the company's stronger cash position, and the shareholder can offset that by selling a few shares.

But very often investors pay attention on dividend policy. There are several reasons [15]:

1) the tax consequences is the first reason for paying or not paying dividends. If tax rules are changed the dividend policy will be changed too. It influences the size of after-tax profit, i.e. profit of shareholders. The management of the company is trying to minimise the tax. And

different types of shareholders (individuals and pension funds) has different tax rules.

2) the positive dividend history of the company is good base to attract funds from capital markets in the future. Potential investors know about size of dividends and can define return.

3) the dividend policy is signal to the market, which do not like cutting dividends. Reduction of dividends or changing the dividend policy very often are bad signals for investors. It means that company has problems.

So, the theory of dividend irrelevance is not completely correct. But it is a good tool for real financial life. Financial theory says that fundamental valuation of the company's activity should usually ignore dividend policy. But from other side, the signalling aspect of theory of dividend irrelevance suggests that dividend yield is an important measure of management confidence. It is a very good indicator of the stability of earnings.

This respect to Crisp plc we can conclude that it is not necessary to change the existing dividend policy. The company has market history, because it is large public firm. Consequently, it has dividend policy. The company considers possibility to attract funds for some profitable investment projects. So, it is normal development of the organization with stable profit.

Words: 2814

4. References

1. Fama, Eugene (1970). "Efficient Capital Markets: A Review of Theory and Empirical Work". Journal of Finance 25: 383–417

2. Sullivan, arthur; Steven M. Sheffrin (2003). Economics: Principles in action. Upper Saddle River,: Pearson Prentice Hall. pp. 283.

3. Saad, Emad W., Student Member, IEEE; Prokhorov, Danil V. Member , IEEE; and Wunsch,II, Donald C. Senior Member, IEEE (November, 1998). "Comparative Study of Stock Trend Prediction Using Time Delay, Recurrent and Probabilistic Neural Networks". IEEE Transactions on Neural Networks 9: 1456–1470.

4. Granger, Clive W. J. & Morgenstern, Oskar (5 May 2007). "Spectral Analysis of New York Stock Market Prices". Kyklos 16 (1): 1–27.

5. Mandelbrot, Benoit & Hudson, Richard L. (2006). The Misbehavior of Markets: A Fractal View of Financial Turbulence, annot. ed.. Basic Books.

6. Taleb, Nassim Nicholas (2008). Fooled by Randomness: The Hidden Role of Chance in Life and in the Markets, 2nd ed. Random House.

7. Dreman David N. & Berry Michael A. (1992). "Overreaction, Underreaction, and the Low-P/E Effect". Financial Analysts Journal 51 (4): 21–30.

8. Ball R. (1978). Anomalies in Relationships between Securities' Yields and Yield-Surrogates. Journal of Financial Economics 6:103-126

9. DeBondt, Werner F.M. & Thaler, Richard H. (1985). "Does the Stock Market Overreact". Journal of Finance 40: 557–558

10. Chopra, Navin; Lakonishok, Josef; & Ritter, Jay R. (1985). "Measuring Abnormal Performance: Do Stocks Overreact". Journal of Financial Economics 31: 235–268.

11. Brealy &al. "Principles of Corporate Finance", Chapter 10

12. 'Overconfidence, Arbitrage, and Equilibrium Asset Pricing,' Kent D. Daniel, David Hirshleifer and Avanidhar Subrahmanyam, Journal of Finance, 56(3) (June, 2001), pp. 921-965

13. Modigliani, F.; Miller, M. (1958). «The Cost of Capital, Corporation Finance and the Theory of Investment»

14. Rosenbaum, Joshua; Joshua Pearl (2009). Investment Banking: Valuation, Leveraged Buyouts, and Mergers & Acquisitions. Hoboken, NJ

15. Yee, Kenton K. (2000). "Aggregation, Dividend Irrelevancy, and Earnings-Value Relations". Contemporary Accounting Research 22 (2): 453–480.